Woodpeckers are birds. They **peck** at trees with their sharp, pointed **beaks**.

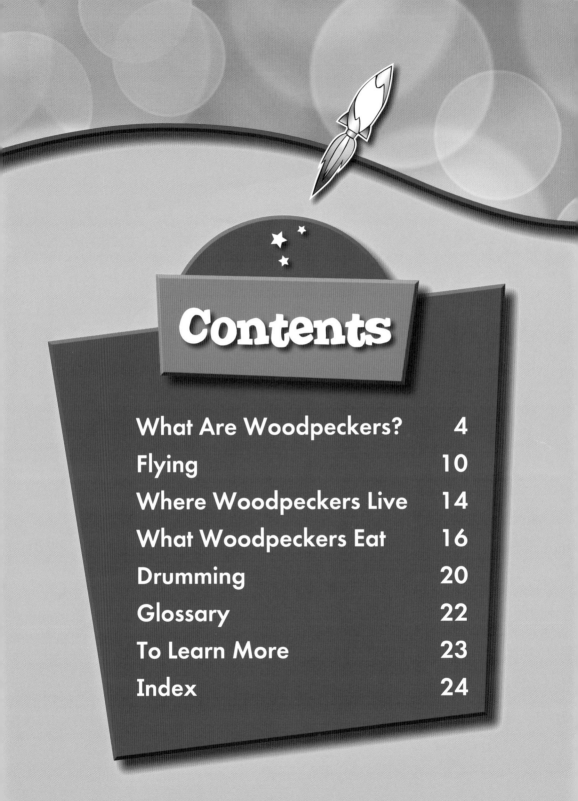

Contents

Woodpeckers have four toes on each foot. Two point forward and two point backward.

Woodpeckers climb straight up trees. Their long, stiff tails help them **balance**.

Woodpeckers fly in a **pattern**. They flap their wings several times and then glide.

Woodpeckers tuck their wings against their bodies when they glide.

Woodpeckers live in forests. They build nests inside trees.

Woodpeckers eat fruits and nuts. They also drill holes into trees to find **insects**.

Woodpeckers stick their long tongues into the holes. They have **barbs** on their tongues to grab insects.

barbs

Woodpeckers **drum** on trees to talk to each other. A male drums to call a female. Tap, tap, tap!

Glossary

balance—to stay steady and not fall

barbs—sharp points; woodpeckers have barbs on their tongues to grab food.

beaks—the mouths of some animals such as birds and turtles

drum—to strike the surface

insects—small animals with six legs and hard outer bodies; insect bodies are divided into three parts.

pattern—a repeated action; when woodpeckers fly, they flap their wings several times and then glide.

peck—to drill into with the beak

To Learn More

AT THE LIBRARY

Murray, Julie. *Woodpeckers*. Edina, Minn.: ABDO Pub. Co., 2005.

Townsend, Emily Rose. *Woodpeckers*. Mankato, Minn.: Capstone Press, 2004.

Wildsmith, Brian. *The Owl and the Woodpecker*. New York, N.Y.: Star Bright Books, 2006.

ON THE WEB

Learning more about woodpeckers is as easy as 1, 2, 3.

1. Go to www.factsurfer.com.

2. Enter "woodpeckers" into the search box.

3. Click the "Surf" button and you will see a list of related Web sites.

With factsurfer.com, finding more information is just a click away.

Index

The images in this book are reproduced through the courtesy of: Minden Pictures/Masterfile, front cover; Tim Zurowski/All Canada Photos/Alamy, p. 5; John Devries/Photolibrary, p. 7; Usher D/Photolibrary, p. 7 (small); Steve Byland, pp. 9, 15; Roland Mayr/Photolibrary, p. 11; Michaela Sagatora, p. 13; Kats Edwin/Arterra Picture Library/Alamy, p. 17; Carlos Caetano, p. 17 (left); Martin Novak, p. 17 (middle); Doug Lemke, p. 17 (right); Kim Taylor/naturepl.com, p. 19; Ted Kinsman/Photo Researchers, Inc., p. 19 (small); Chris O'Reilly/naturepl.com, p. 21.

10/18-2(7/18)

PRESIDENTIAL PERSPECTIVES

WORLD WAR II
THROUGH THE EYES OF
FRANKLIN DELANO ROOSEVELT

by Kate Conley

Content Consultant
Peter Vermilyea
History Department
Western Connecticut State University

Core Library

An Imprint of Abdo Publishing
abdopublishing.com

abdopublishing.com

Published by Abdo Publishing, a division of ABDO, PO Box 398166, Minneapolis, Minnesota 55439. Copyright © 2016 by Abdo Consulting Group, Inc. International copyrights reserved in all countries. No part of this book may be reproduced in any form without written permission from the publisher. Core Library™ is a trademark and logo of Abdo Publishing.

Printed in the United States of America, North Mankato, Minnesota
082015
012016

THIS BOOK CONTAINS
RECYCLED MATERIALS

Cover Photo: Bettmann/Corbis
Interior Photos: Bettmann/Corbis, 1, 11, 26, 28, 32, 40; AP Images, 4, 8, 12, 16, 23, 34, 36, 45; British Official Photo/AP Images, 18; Red Line Editorial, 21; Kingendai/AFLO/Nippon News/ Corbis, 24

Editor: Jon Westmark
Series Designer: Laura Polzin

Library of Congress Control Number: 2015945415

Cataloging-in-Publication Data
Conley, Kate.
 World War II through the eyes of Franklin Delano Roosevelt / Kate Conley.
   p. cm. -- (Presidential perspectives)
ISBN 978-1-68078-036-9 (lib. bdg.)
Includes bibliographical references and index.
1. World War, 1939-1945--Juvenile literature.   2. Roosevelt, Franklin D. (Franklin Delano), 1882-1945--Juvenile literature.   3. Presidents--United States--Juvenile literature.   I. Title.
973.9--dc23

                                                                    2015945415